**W9-BTZ-002**

CHECKERBOARD BIOGRAPHY LIBRARY

U.S. PRESIDENTS

*The*
*United States Presidents*

# MARTIN VAN BUREN

ABDO Publishing Company

BreAnn Rumsch

# visit us at
# www.abdopublishing.com

Cover Photo: Getty Images
Interior Photos: Alamy p. 26; Corbis pp. 11, 13, 28, 29; iStockphoto p. 32; Library of Congress pp. 5,
    9, 14, 15, 17, 19, 23, 24, 27; North Wind p. 12; Picture History pp. 18, 21, 25

Editor: Megan M. Gunderson
Art Direction & Cover Design: Neil Klinepier
Interior Design: Neil Klinepier

## Library of Congress Cataloging-in-Publication Data

Rumsch, BreAnn, 1981-
  Martin Van Buren / BreAnn Rumsch.
     p. cm. --  (The United States presidents)
  Includes index.
  ISBN 978-1-60453-478-8
  1. Van Buren, Martin, 1782-1862--Juvenile literature. 2. Presidents--United States--Biography--
Juvenile literature.  I. Title.
  E387.R86 2009
  973.5'7092--dc22
  [B]
                                        2008037924

# CONTENTS

# MARTIN VAN BUREN

Martin Van Buren was the eighth president of the United States. As a young man, he became a lawyer. Then, he began his career in politics.

Van Buren served in many public offices. He was a New York state senator and a U.S. senator. He was also elected governor of New York. Van Buren later served as **secretary of state** and vice president. Then in 1836, he was elected president.

As president, Van Buren handled many challenging situations. He led the country through the Panic of 1837. Van Buren also worked to keep peace with Great Britain and Canada.

President Van Buren established an independent **treasury**. And, he fought against the spread of slavery. However, he also forced Native Americans off their lands.

Van Buren ran for president two more times. Yet, he was never reelected. Even so, he continued to work in politics for many years.

Throughout his life, Van Buren was an important American leader. He is best remembered for two main contributions to politics. Van Buren founded America's first political **machine**, and he organized the **Democratic** Party.

# TIMELINE

**1782** - On December 5, Martin Van Buren was born in Kinderhook, New York.

**1796** - Van Buren began working as an apprentice for a lawyer named Francis Silvester.

**1807** - On February 21, Van Buren married Hannah Hoes.

**1812** - Van Buren was elected to the New York senate.

**1816** - Van Buren was reelected state senator; New York governor Daniel D. Tompkins made him attorney general.

**1819** - Hannah Van Buren died in February.

**1821** - Van Buren won election to the U.S. Senate.

**1828** - Van Buren was elected governor of New York.

**1829** - President Andrew Jackson appointed Van Buren secretary of state.

**1833** - Van Buren became vice president under President Jackson.

**1837** - On March 4, Van Buren became the eighth U.S. president; the United States faced the Panic of 1837; Texas applied to become a state.

**1838** - The U.S. government forced Cherokee Native Americans from their homelands to present-day Oklahoma.

**1840** - On July 4, Congress passed the Independent Treasury Act; Van Buren ran for reelection but lost.

**1848** - The Free-Soil Party nominated Van Buren for president, but he lost the election.

**1862** - On July 24, Martin Van Buren died at Lindenwald in Kinderhook.

# DID YOU KNOW?

The Martin Van Buren National Historic Site was founded in 1974. The site is located in Kinderhook, New York. It includes Van Buren's mansion, Lindenwald, and about 40 acres (16 ha) of land.

The White House has been redecorated many times. However, the tradition of the Blue Room began while Van Buren was president. He redecorated this oval reception room in the color that remains today.

For his careful political scheming, Van Buren's friends called him the "Little Magician." His enemies called him the "Red Fox of Kinderhook."

In the 1836 election, the U.S. Senate chose Van Buren's vice president. No other vice president in U.S. history has been selected by the Senate.

# KINDERHOOK YOUTH

Martin Van Buren was born in Kinderhook, New York, on December 5, 1782.  He was the first president born a U.S. citizen. All previous presidents had been born before the **Declaration of Independence** was signed.  So, they were born as British subjects.

Martin's parents were Abraham and Maria Hoes Van Buren. Abraham ran a farm and owned a tavern.  Maria managed the household.

The Van Buren family was large.  Martin was the third of Abraham and Maria's five children.  He also had two half brothers and one half sister.

As a boy, Martin liked to go fishing.  He also enjoyed attending local theater performances.  When it was time to receive his education, Martin attended the village school in Kinderhook.  There, he learned reading, writing, and some Latin.

## FAST FACTS

**BORN** - December 5, 1782
**WIFE** - Hannah Hoes
     (1783–1819)
**CHILDREN** - 4
**POLITICAL PARTY** - Democrat
**AGE AT INAUGURATION** - 54
**YEARS SERVED** - 1837–1841
**VICE PRESIDENT** - Richard M. Johnson
**DIED** - July 24, 1862, age 79

8

*Martin's birthplace was also the site of his father's tavern.*
*Today, all that remains is a historical marker.*

Martin also helped his father on the farm and in the tavern. While working in the tavern, Martin met lawyers, businessmen, and politicians. He often listened to them talk. In this way, Martin learned about current events around the world.

# LEARNING THE LAW

In 1796, Van Buren became an **apprentice**. He worked for a lawyer named Francis Silvester. Van Buren kept the office clean and worked as Silvester's law clerk.

Silvester belonged to the Federalist Party. This party favored a strong national government. It also supported laws that would help wealthy people. Silvester wanted Van Buren to be a Federalist, too.

However, Van Buren agreed with the **Democratic-Republican** Party instead. It favored a government that would help the common people.

In 1801, Van Buren was ready for a change. So, he traveled to New York City, New York. There, he completed his law studies under William P. Van Ness.

Van Buren passed his law examination in 1803. Now he could work as a lawyer. He joined his half brother James Van Alen at a law office in Kinderhook. Van Buren became a partner at the firm.

Soon, Van Buren was ready to marry. On February 21, 1807, he married Hannah Hoes. She was a distant cousin. She was also Van Buren's childhood sweetheart.

The next year, their first son was born. They named him Abraham. The Van Burens eventually had three more sons named John, Martin Jr., and Smith. Van Buren raised his sons alone after Hannah Van Buren died in February 1819.

*Hannah Van Buren*

# NEW YORK LEADER

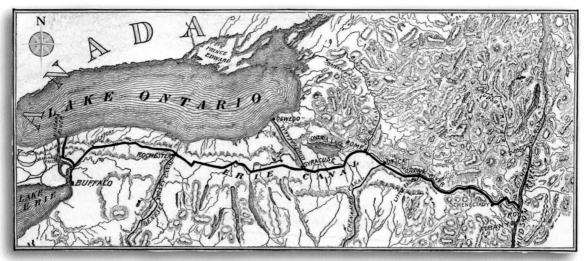

*The Erie Canal connects New York City, New York, to the Great Lakes by way of the Hudson River.*

In 1808, Van Buren got his first job in politics. He became surrogate of Columbia County, New York. Van Buren worked hard at his new job.

As surrogate, Van Buren worked with the county's landowners. He settled disagreements over estates and property rights. This allowed him to meet many powerful New Yorkers.

Van Buren was elected to the New York senate in 1812. Senator Van Buren supported the **War of 1812**. He wanted to help

protect the United States from Great Britain. So, he wrote a bill to send men into the army. It promised 12,000 men from the New York **militia**.

Van Buren was reelected state senator in 1816. That year, he supported a bill to build the Erie Canal. It would improve transportation and business in New York. Also in 1816, New York governor Daniel D. Tompkins made Van Buren **attorney general**. Van Buren held both positions for several years.

*The Erie Canal was completed in 1825. It was an instant success!*

# VAN BUREN'S MACHINE

While serving in the senate, Van Buren led a group of **Democratic-Republicans** called the bucktails. They did not agree with New York City mayor DeWitt Clinton's policies.

So, the bucktails were upset when Clinton was elected governor of New York in 1817. Two years later, Clinton removed Van Buren from his job as **attorney general**.

*DeWitt Clinton served as governor of New York from 1817 to 1822. He also served from 1825 to 1828.*

Van Buren and the bucktails continued to disagree with Clinton. They did not want him to be governor any longer. However, New Yorkers reelected Clinton in 1820.

Meanwhile, Senator Van Buren had been working for several years to create a new political system. He hoped it would make the **Democratic-Republican** Party more powerful.

Using the spoils system, Van Buren helped put party supporters in state government jobs. As more bucktails were hired, the Democratic-Republican Party's power grew. Soon,

*Van Buren's Albany Regency lasted for nearly 30 years.*

Van Buren's supporters formed America's first political **machine**. The group was called the Albany Regency.

The Albany Regency's votes controlled the party's nominations. So in 1821, Van Buren was easily nominated to run for the U.S. Senate. He won the election! Soon, he was off to Washington, D.C.

# TO THE CAPITOL

Van Buren was a U.S. senator from 1821 to 1828. During that time, he served on the Committee on Finance. He was also chairman of the Committee on the **Judiciary**. Senator Van Buren did not speak often. But, he could argue well and knew his facts.

As a senator, Van Buren worked to end **debtors**' prison. People went to this prison if they owed large amounts of money. Van Buren felt it was unfair to jail people just for being poor.

Van Buren also tried to stop the slave trade. He wrote a bill that said no one could buy any more slaves. Yet, it allowed people who already owned slaves to keep them. The bill was defeated.

In 1828, Van Buren was elected governor of New York. He took office in January 1829. However, he would not remain there long.

As governor, Van Buren supported the Safety Fund Plan. Under this program, banks were required to set aside money for emergencies. Banks also had to limit the amount of paper money they issued. This helped protect the value of money.

In March 1829, Andrew Jackson became president. He appointed Van Buren his **secretary of state**. So, Van Buren left the governorship.

As secretary of state, Van Buren successfully made treaties with other countries. In 1830, Turkey agreed to allow U.S. ships to sail in the Black Sea. That same year, Great Britain agreed to allow the United States to trade in the West Indies.

*Andrew Jackson was president from 1829 to 1837.*

**DEMOCRATIC TICKET.**

FOR PRESIDENT,
*MARTIN VAN BUREN.*
FOR VICE PRESIDENT,
*RICHARD M. JOHNSON.*

OHIO ELECTORS.
John M. Goodenow,
Othniel Looker,
Jacob Felter,
James B. Cameron,
David S. Davis,
James Fife,
John J. Higgins,
Joseph Morris,
James Sharp,
John McElvain,
William Trevitt,
David Robb,
Hugh McComb,
Robert Mitchell,
James Mathews,
Joshua Seney,
Stephen N. Sargent,
Thomas J. McLain,
Noah Frederick,
Jacob Ihrig,
James Means.

Van Buren was an important adviser to President Jackson. He encouraged the president to use the spoils system. Van Buren was also a leader in Jackson's Kitchen **Cabinet**. Most of these advisers did not work in Jackson's regular cabinet.

In 1831, Van Buren resigned as **secretary of state**. Jackson tried to appoint him minister to Great Britain. However, the Senate rejected Van Buren's appointment to this position.

Meanwhile, the **Democratic-Republican** Party had split in two. Van Buren, Jackson, and others favored strong state governments and a small federal government. They formed what became known as the **Democratic** Party. Those who disagreed with these ideas formed what became the **Whig** Party.

*A Democratic election ticket shows Van Buren as a magician. Democrats believed he would provide liberty and equal rights.*

In 1832, President Jackson was up for reelection. **Democrats** chose Van Buren to run as his **running mate**. Jackson's opponents nominated Senator Henry Clay to run for president. Jackson won the election! So, Van Buren became vice president on March 4, 1833.

In 1836, Van Buren decided to run

*Richard M. Johnson*

for president. Jackson supported his campaign. Van Buren faced three opponents from the **Whig** Party. They were William H. Harrison, Daniel Webster, and Hugh L. White. Van Buren won the election with 170 electoral votes to Harrison's 73.

No candidate for vice president won a majority of the electoral votes. So, the U.S. Senate chose the winner. Kentucky representative Richard M. Johnson became Van Buren's vice president.

# PRESIDENT VAN BUREN

Van Buren was **inaugurated** on March 4, 1837. Shortly after, the Panic of 1837 began. It was the first great depression in U.S. history. Banks ran out of money, and people lost their jobs. President Van Buren believed some banks had caused this depression. He felt they had used government money carelessly.

President Van Buren asked Congress to form an independent **treasury**. It would give the government control over which banks had access to federal money. Van Buren believed his plan would prevent another depression. However, Congress voted against forming the treasury.

Meanwhile, Texas had declared its independence from Mexico. In summer 1837, Texas applied to become a state. President Van Buren worried that **annexing** Texas would lead to war with Mexico.

In addition, annexing Texas would raise the question of slavery. Some Americans would want to allow slavery in Texas. But many would not. Van Buren did not want to divide the country. So, he did not annex Texas.

*Angelica Singleton Van Buren was Van Buren's daughter-in-law. She served as White House hostess during his presidency.*

In late 1837, President Van Buren faced problems with Canada. The Canadians wanted independence from Great Britain. Some Americans wanted to help the Canadians. So, they sent a supply ship called the *Caroline* to Canada.

In December, British soldiers ordered an attack on the ship. Several Americans onboard were wounded and one was killed. Still, Van Buren needed to avoid war with Great Britain. So, he issued a message. It stated that America would not take sides in the conflict.

Meanwhile, white settlers had been moving west and taking over Native American lands. In 1838, the U.S. government forced Cherokee Native Americans to leave their homelands. They were sent to a **reservation** in present-day Oklahoma. They traveled nearly 1,000 miles (1,600 km) to get there. Thousands of Cherokee died on the journey. It became known as the Trail of Tears.

At the same time, U.S. troops were fighting Seminole Native Americans in Florida. White Americans wanted the Seminole tribe's land there. The Second Seminole War lasted from 1835 to 1842. The war was costly. And, thousands of Americans and Seminoles died.

# PRESIDENT VAN BUREN'S CABINET

MARCH 4, 1837–
MARCH 4, 1841

- **STATE –** John Forsyth
- **TREASURY –** Levi Woodbury
- **WAR –** Joel Roberts Poinsett
- **NAVY –** Mahlon Dickerson
  James Kirke Paulding (from July 1, 1838)
- **ATTORNEY GENERAL –** Benjamin Franklin Butler
  Felix Grundy (from September 1, 1838)
  Henry Dilworth Gilpin (from January 11, 1840)

In 1839, Van Buren faced more problems with Canada. The United States and Canada disagreed about the border between Maine and New Brunswick.

To avoid war, President Van Buren sent General Winfield Scott to the area. Scott made an agreement with British officials. Both countries would occupy the land until a formal decision could be reached. The Webster-Ashburton Treaty of 1842 later established the permanent boundary line.

Meanwhile, President Van Buren continued to fight Congress for an independent **treasury**. On July 4, 1840, Congress finally passed the Independent Treasury Act.

## SUPREME COURT APPOINTMENTS

**JOHN CATRON** - 1837
**JOHN MᶜKINLEY** - 1838
**PETER V. DANIEL** - 1842

24

*Van Buren called the independent treasury bill a "second declaration of independence."*

Also in 1840, Van Buren ran for reelection. The **Democrats** could not agree on a candidate for vice president. So, Van Buren ran without a **running mate**. He became the only president in U.S. history to do so.

The **Whigs** nominated Harrison for president once more. They named former senator John Tyler of Virginia as his running mate.

Some of the events in Van Buren's presidency had made him unpopular. This cost him many votes. So, Van Buren lost the election to Harrison.

# LIFELONG POLITICIAN

*Van Buren named his estate Lindenwald after the many linden trees on the property.*

Van Buren left the White House in March 1841. He retired to Lindenwald, his country estate in Kinderhook. However, Van Buren continued to work in politics. In 1844, he decided to run for president again.

Van Buren still opposed expanding the number of slave states in the country. So, he still did not want to **annex** Texas. Many **Democrats** disagreed with him. They wanted to annex Texas and make the United States larger.

Van Buren's views made him unpopular within his party. So, he did not win the Democratic nomination for president. Instead,

*James K. Polk was president from 1845 to 1849.*

the party nominated James K. Polk. Polk became president in 1845.

That year, the United States annexed Texas. This caused the Democratic Party to split into two groups. They were known as the hunkers and the barnburners.

*In the 1848 election, Van Buren won just 10 percent of the popular vote. However, he drew votes away from the Democratic ticket, securing Taylor's victory.*

Van Buren led the barnburners. They wanted to stop slavery from spreading. In 1848, the barnburners formed the **Free-Soil** Party. That year, they nominated Van Buren to run for president.

The **Whig** Party nominated Zachary Taylor for president. The **Democrats** nominated Lewis Cass for president. Van Buren's strong views against slavery upset many Americans. So, he lost the election to Taylor.

For the next several years, Van Buren traveled around Europe. He returned to Kinderhook in 1855. There, he tended to his farms and continued to follow national politics. He also wrote a book about his life in politics. It is called *Autobiography*. Martin Van Buren died at Lindenwald on July 24, 1862.

Van Buren worked his way from county surrogate to U.S. president. He faced many challenges during his presidency. These included the Panic of 1837 and conflicts with Canada and Native Americans. Martin Van Buren also made important contributions to politics. He helped organize the **Democratic** Party and remained loyal to it throughout his life.

*Van Buren is buried beside his wife in the Kinderhook cemetery.*

# OFFICE OF THE PRESIDENT

## BRANCHES OF GOVERNMENT

The U.S. government is divided into three branches. They are the executive, legislative, and judicial branches. This division is called a separation of powers. Each branch has some power over the others. This is called a system of checks and balances.

### EXECUTIVE BRANCH

The executive branch enforces laws. It is made up of the president, the vice president, and the president's cabinet. The president represents the United States around the world. He or she oversees relations with other countries and signs treaties. The president signs bills into law and appoints officials and federal judges. He or she also leads the military and manages government workers.

### LEGISLATIVE BRANCH

The legislative branch makes laws, maintains the military, and regulates trade. It also has the power to declare war. This branch consists of the Senate and the House of Representatives. Together, these two houses make up Congress. Each state has two senators. A state's population determines the number of representatives it has.

### JUDICIAL BRANCH

The judicial branch interprets laws. It consists of district courts, courts of appeals, and the Supreme Court. District courts try cases. If a person disagrees with a trial's outcome, he or she may appeal. If the courts of appeals support the ruling, a person may appeal to the Supreme Court. The Supreme Court also makes sure that laws follow the U.S. Constitution.

# Qualifications for Office

To be president, a person must meet three requirements. A candidate must be at least 35 years old and a natural-born U.S. citizen. He or she must also have lived in the United States for at least 14 years.

# Electoral College

The U.S. presidential election is an indirect election. Voters from each state choose electors to represent them in the Electoral College. The number of electors from each state is based on population. Each elector has one electoral vote. Electors are pledged to cast their vote for the candidate who receives the highest number of popular votes in their state. A candidate must receive the majority of Electoral College votes to win.

# Term of Office

Each president may be elected to two four-year terms. Sometimes, a president may only be elected once. This happens if he or she served more than two years of the previous president's term.

The presidential election is held on the Tuesday after the first Monday in November. The president is sworn in on January 20 of the following year. At that time, he or she takes the oath of office:

I do solemnly swear (or affirm) that I will faithfully execute the office of President of the United States, and will to the best of my ability, preserve, protect and defend the Constitution of the United States.

# LINE OF SUCCESSION

The Presidential Succession Act of 1947 defines who becomes president if the president cannot serve. The vice president is first in the line of succession. Next are the Speaker of the House and the President Pro Tempore of the Senate. If none of these individuals is able to serve, the office falls to the president's cabinet members. They would take office in the order in which each department was created:

Secretary of State

Secretary of the Treasury

Secretary of Defense

Attorney General

Secretary of the Interior

Secretary of Agriculture

Secretary of Commerce

Secretary of Labor

Secretary of Health and Human Services

Secretary of Housing and Urban Development

Secretary of Transportation

Secretary of Energy

Secretary of Education

Secretary of Veterans Affairs

Secretary of Homeland Security

# BENEFITS

- While in office, the president receives a salary of $400,000 each year. He or she lives in the White House and has 24-hour Secret Service protection.

- The president may travel on a Boeing 747 jet called Air Force One. The airplane can accommodate 70 passengers. It has kitchens, a dining room, sleeping areas, and a conference room. It also has fully equipped offices with the latest communications systems. Air Force One can fly halfway around the world before needing to refuel. It can even refuel in flight!

- If the president wishes to travel by car, he or she uses Cadillac One. Cadillac One is a Cadillac Deville. It has been modified with heavy armor and communications systems. The president takes Cadillac One along when visiting other countries if secure transportation will be needed.

- The president also travels on a helicopter called Marine One. Like the presidential car, Marine One accompanies the president when traveling abroad if necessary.

- Sometimes, the president needs to get away and relax with family and friends. Camp David is the official presidential retreat. It is located in the cool, wooded mountains in Maryland. The U.S. Navy maintains the retreat, and the U.S. Marine Corps keeps it secure. The camp offers swimming, tennis, golf, and hiking.

- When the president leaves office, he or she receives Secret Service protection for ten more years. He or she also receives a yearly pension of $191,300 and funding for office space, supplies, and staff.

# PRESIDENTS AND THEIR TERMS

| PRESIDENT | PARTY | TOOK OFFICE | LEFT OFFICE | TERMS SERVED | VICE PRESIDENT |
|---|---|---|---|---|---|
| George Washington | None | April 30, 1789 | March 4, 1797 | Two | John Adams |
| John Adams | Federalist | March 4, 1797 | March 4, 1801 | One | Thomas Jefferson |
| Thomas Jefferson | Democratic-Republican | March 4, 1801 | March 4, 1809 | Two | Aaron Burr, George Clinton |
| James Madison | Democratic-Republican | March 4, 1809 | March 4, 1817 | Two | George Clinton, Elbridge Gerry |
| James Monroe | Democratic-Republican | March 4, 1817 | March 4, 1825 | Two | Daniel D. Tompkins |
| John Quincy Adams | Democratic-Republican | March 4, 1825 | March 4, 1829 | One | John C. Calhoun |
| Andrew Jackson | Democrat | March 4, 1829 | March 4, 1837 | Two | John C. Calhoun, Martin Van Buren |
| Martin Van Buren | Democrat | March 4, 1837 | March 4, 1841 | One | Richard M. Johnson |
| William H. Harrison | Whig | March 4, 1841 | April 4, 1841 | Died During First Term | John Tyler |
| John Tyler | Whig | April 6, 1841 | March 4, 1845 | Completed Harrison's Term | Office Vacant |
| James K. Polk | Democrat | March 4, 1845 | March 4, 1849 | One | George M. Dallas |
| Zachary Taylor | Whig | March 5, 1849 | July 9, 1850 | Died During First Term | Millard Fillmore |

PRESIDENTS 1–12, 1789–1850

| PRESIDENT | PARTY | TOOK OFFICE | LEFT OFFICE | TERMS SERVED | VICE PRESIDENT |
|---|---|---|---|---|---|
| Millard Fillmore | Whig | July 10, 1850 | March 4, 1853 | Completed Taylor's Term | Office Vacant |
| Franklin Pierce | Democrat | March 4, 1853 | March 4, 1857 | One | William R.D. King |
| James Buchanan | Democrat | March 4, 1857 | March 4, 1861 | One | John C. Breckinridge |
| Abraham Lincoln | Republican | March 4, 1861 | April 15, 1865 | Served One Term, Died During Second Term | Hannibal Hamlin, Andrew Johnson |
| Andrew Johnson | Democrat | April 15, 1865 | March 4, 1869 | Completed Lincoln's Second Term | Office Vacant |
| Ulysses S. Grant | Republican | March 4, 1869 | March 4, 1877 | Two | Schuyler Colfax, Henry Wilson |
| Rutherford B. Hayes | Republican | March 3, 1877 | March 4, 1881 | One | William A. Wheeler |
| James A. Garfield | Republican | March 4, 1881 | September 19, 1881 | Died During First Term | Chester Arthur |
| Chester Arthur | Republican | September 20, 1881 | March 4, 1885 | Completed Garfield's Term | Office Vacant |
| Grover Cleveland | Democrat | March 4, 1885 | March 4, 1889 | One | Thomas A. Hendricks |
| Benjamin Harrison | Republican | March 4, 1889 | March 4, 1893 | One | Levi P. Morton |
| Grover Cleveland | Democrat | March 4, 1893 | March 4, 1897 | One | Adlai E. Stevenson |
| William McKinley | Republican | March 4, 1897 | September 14, 1901 | Served One Term, Died During Second Term | Garret A. Hobart, Theodore Roosevelt |

| PRESIDENT | PARTY | TOOK OFFICE | LEFT OFFICE | TERMS SERVED | VICE PRESIDENT |
|---|---|---|---|---|---|
| **Theodore Roosevelt** | Republican | September 14, 1901 | March 4, 1909 | Completed McKinley's Second Term, Served One Term | Office Vacant, Charles Fairbanks |
| **William Taft** | Republican | March 4, 1909 | March 4, 1913 | One | James S. Sherman |
| **Woodrow Wilson** | Democrat | March 4, 1913 | March 4, 1921 | Two | Thomas R. Marshall |
| **Warren G. Harding** | Republican | March 4, 1921 | August 2, 1923 | Died During First Term | Calvin Coolidge |
| **Calvin Coolidge** | Republican | August 3, 1923 | March 4, 1929 | Completed Harding's Term, Served One Term | Office Vacant, Charles Dawes |
| **Herbert Hoover** | Republican | March 4, 1929 | March 4, 1933 | One | Charles Curtis |
| **Franklin D. Roosevelt** | Democrat | March 4, 1933 | April 12, 1945 | Served Three Terms, Died During Fourth Term | John Nance Garner, Henry A. Wallace, Harry S. Truman |
| **Harry S. Truman** | Democrat | April 12, 1945 | January 20, 1953 | Completed Roosevelt's Fourth Term, Served One Term | Office Vacant, Alben Barkley |
| **Dwight D. Eisenhower** | Republican | January 20, 1953 | January 20, 1961 | Two | Richard Nixon |
| **John F. Kennedy** | Democrat | January 20, 1961 | November 22, 1963 | Died During First Term | Lyndon B. Johnson |
| **Lyndon B. Johnson** | Democrat | November 22, 1963 | January 20, 1969 | Completed Kennedy's Term, Served One Term | Office Vacant, Hubert H. Humphrey |
| **Richard Nixon** | Republican | January 20, 1969 | August 9, 1974 | Completed First Term, Resigned During Second Term | Spiro T. Agnew, Gerald Ford |

PRESIDENTS 26–37, 1901–1974

| PRESIDENT | PARTY | TOOK OFFICE | LEFT OFFICE | TERMS SERVED | VICE PRESIDENT |
|---|---|---|---|---|---|
| Gerald Ford | Republican | August 9, 1974 | January 20, 1977 | Completed Nixon's Second Term | Nelson A. Rockefeller |
| Jimmy Carter | Democrat | January 20, 1977 | January 20, 1981 | One | Walter Mondale |
| Ronald Reagan | Republican | January 20, 1981 | January 20, 1989 | Two | George H.W. Bush |
| George H.W. Bush | Republican | January 20, 1989 | January 20, 1993 | One | Dan Quayle |
| Bill Clinton | Democrat | January 20, 1993 | January 20, 2001 | Two | Al Gore |
| George W. Bush | Republican | January 20, 2001 | January 20, 2009 | Two | Dick Cheney |
| Barack Obama | Democrat | January 20, 2009 | | | Joe Biden |

*"The less government interferes, the better for general prosperity." Martin Van Buren*

# WRITE TO THE PRESIDENT

You may write to the president at:

**The White House
1600 Pennsylvania Avenue NW
Washington, DC 20500**

You may e-mail the president at:

**comments@whitehouse.gov**

# GLOSSARY

**annex** - to take land and add it to a nation.

**apprentice** - a person who learns a trade or a craft from a skilled worker.

**attorney general** - the chief law officer of a national or state government.

**cabinet** - a group of advisers chosen by the president to lead government departments.

**debtor** - someone who owes something, usually money, to someone.

**Declaration of Independence** - an essay written at the Second Continental Congress in 1776, announcing the separation of the American colonies from England.

**Democrat** - a member of the Democratic political party. When Martin Van Buren was president, Democrats supported farmers and landowners.

**Democratic-Republican** - a member of the Democratic-Republican political party. During the early 1800s, Democratic-Republicans believed in weak national government and strong state government.

**Free-Soil** - a political party that had power between 1848 and 1854. Its members opposed the extension of slavery into U.S. territories and the admission of slave states into the Union.

**inaugurate** (ih-NAW-gyuh-rayt) - to swear into a political office.

**judiciary** (joo-DIH-shee-ehr-ee) - the branch of a government in charge of courts and judges.

**machine** - a highly organized political group under the leadership of a boss.

**militia** (muh-LIH-shuh) - a group of citizens trained for war or emergencies.

**reservation** - a piece of land set aside by the government for Native Americans to live on.

**running mate** - a candidate running for a lower-rank position on an election ticket, especially the candidate for vice president.

**secretary of state** - a member of the president's cabinet who handles relations with other countries.

**treasury** - a place where money is kept.

**War of 1812** - from 1812 to 1814. A war fought between the United States and Great Britain over shipping rights and the capture of U.S. soldiers.

**Whig** - a member of a political party that was very strong in the early 1800s but ended in the 1850s. Whigs supported laws that helped business.

# WEB SITES

To learn more about Martin Van Buren, visit ABDO Publishing Company on the World Wide Web at **www.abdopublishing.com**. Web sites about Martin Van Buren are featured on our Book Links page. These links are routinely monitored and updated to provide the most current information available.

# INDEX

J B VANBUREN

**Rumsch, BreAnn.**
**Martin Van Buren**

SOF

R4002310906